Dramatic Irony

Nicholette A. Guy

BookLeaf
Publishing

India | USA | UK

Presentation by *BookLeaf Publishing*

Web: www.bookleafpub.com

E-mail: info@bookleafpub.com

ISBN: 9789357215459

First edition 2022

This book is dedicated to everyone afraid their changes are not helping. You are improving your life day by day, and I see you.

ACKNOWLEDGEMENT

My partner helps in more ways that I know how to express. Without him, I might still be stuck in the toxic cycles of others, lost in provocation and volatility.

My writing community has been a saving grace. Before them, I had never felt like I'd fit in anywhere with anyone. Thank you for your support and listening to me when I'm panicking about my abilities and life choices. Thank you for validating me as a writer and reading my shitty drafts. I can't wait to read your stories in print one day.

Thank you to the universe for putting amazing people on my path and supporting me on my journey through the ether.

PREFACE

Dear reader,

In writing these poems, I explored buried parts of myself and poked holes in what I had believed to be true. Together, they tell the story of my life and my mental state. Over the year of 2022, I hit lows and highs. My anxiety, depression, and need for perfection crippled me in the beginning of the year as I wrote through my imposter syndrome. About midway through the year, I embraced myself and my tide began to shift and fill. I finished writing two first drafts and made the intention of bettering my physical fitness.

The journey through healing is not linear nor paved with flowers. I hope you read these poems and find strength in not being alone.

Wishing all the best,

Nicholette A. Guy

2022

Autopilot off
Shallow breathing
Strained thinking

Restoration asks the question
How'd you fuck this up so bad?

I don't have any answers
Just questions to questions

One day turned into years
Now my ass numbs beneath my weight
Movement a chore
Taking the place of a clean room

Therapy increased my insanity
By proving my sanity
Now I sit alone
With toxicity oozing from the walls

Freedom isn't all it's cracked up to be
But how can we ever really be free?

Look at how blind we are
Staring at ourselves, yelling at ourselves

When we sit down together
Is the peace we share
As fake as everything else?

Forgiveness

Shapes dance across my vision
Pounding headaches
Amplified by rasping breath
And roiling insides
Let me out, they say

Can't you see I'm trying?

With growing dots
Seeing ceases
Signals of bodily rejection

Has my body rejected me
Or have I rejected it?

Sorry for the damage I've done
Forgive me

Tomorrow will be better

Changing

Life moves on
Despite your best wishes
Or maybe beyond your wildest

Change accompanies each step
Forward and backward
Left and right
Down and up

Now I'm just saying things

Things you don't want to hear
No one wants to change
They only wish for the end result

Would you do what it takes?
To change your life
To change your mind
To change your body

I would

But again I'm human
So I don't really want to

I just do what's easy

I'm the same as you
Even if you don't see it
Even if you don't see me
Even if you don't like me

That's okay

I like you anyway

Acceptance

I'm blind
Yet darkness eludes me
In its place
Manufactured light

I've learned to be a miss
Despite the implications
Replacing your expectations
With my own reality

Identity is fleeting
But only for the broken
The damaged
Those that are forced

I called out for help
But maybe I wasn't loud enough
The response was always silence
Echoing across the years

I'm sorry for my ignorance
Despite my attempts
I didn't see you, hear you
Feel you, understand you

I was never all that different
Yet I fought to be
Now I'm here for you
If you'll have me

Purpose

Apathy
Best described as
Dead inside

Emotions lowered
Worry high

For what?

The illusion

Life isn't listening

It pulls and pulls
Tugging at what's left

What more do you have to give?

Is there any reason for it?

A purpose?

Do I have one?

I wish I had a purpose

I wish we all did

Instead we're set here
To live then die

There is no afterlife

Another lie
To beat you into conformity

I was there once
Then I left

All that stands with me
For me
Is me

The universe
Pulling us all
Down a set path

I do not believe
Freewill exists
Because its existence
Would insinuate
That we matter

That all of this matters

But how can that be

Without purpose

Trapped

If only my moods were less
Mundane
I could enrapture you
With words

Pull you into a world
You know and understand

I deal in the currency of moments
My moments exist in bubbles
A bubble I don't know how to leave anymore
My days repeat within the same sphere
I only breach out
In new places

When did it get this way?
How did I end up here?
Stuck in a repetitive cycle
Like the habitual creature
I really am
Habits no more good than bad

The biggest difference between me and some
Is that I have so much time to see it as it is

I don't have filler time
My time is dedicated in blocks across my day
One bleeds into the next

There is no commute
No space
No breath

I exist in a place
Outside the flow of movement

How could I exist within
When everything is without

In stillness
There is time for deliberation
Time for contemplation and overthinking

Two things I don't need
Two things that magnify
My anxiety
Socially and personally

I miss the need to be somewhere else
To be with others
Even when I don't want to be

The need for an alternative location
Instead I'm stuck here

With no place to go

When I push against the bounds of the bubble
The bubble pushes back
The anxiety pushes in
And I crush inwards

Touched

There were times I thought the moments would
stay forever
Fingerprints creating permanent craters in my
skin

What I didn't understand
Was that those fingerprints
Had already slipped through
Nuzzled in like a parasite
Burying themselves in a forgotten chamber
A chamber only opening in darker moments
Either for inviting more in
Or for me to shine light on the ramifications

Of the consequences brought forth
From skin to skin

Unpacking

The crack in the mask
    Broke through the barrier
        A barrier that kept me safe
            Or so I thought

Turns out my pretending
    Wasn't protecting me
        It was protecting them
            Those that wronged me
            Had hurt me

By keeping my mouth shut
    I allowed them to grow
        To keep their hold on me
            They needed my silence
            My cooperation

I became more and more
    Confused
        My questions centered around
            What did I do wrong?

But that was the goal wasn't it?
    To make sure I felt crazy
        Because when you feel crazy

                        You start acting a little
crazy

You start to believe maybe you are
        Crazy
                Crazy enough to yell when it's
too much
                Crazy enough to feel like there's
something wrong
                Crazy enough to stand in front
of a room of people who were
supposed to love you and yell
Enough

Yeah, maybe I am a little crazy,
        Crazy for keeping your secrets
                Crazy for believing the words
                        Blasting out of your
mouth

And as each of those bullets hit me
        I was crazy enough to believe them

16

Gaslit

I keep waiting for the changes I'm making to
show
Like butterfly wings will sprout from my back

Instead improvements hang above my head in a
rain cloud
Following me into each room
Following me even in my better days
Days that are just okay really
Born from a set of unrealistic expectations

They told me what I feel
They told me how to feel
They told me to forget I feel anything

How can you forget the constant disappointment
raining down on you?

There's no gem in the sand
The gems are eyes of the snake
They wish to mislead you
Pull you towards the hole they created for you
With you
The eyes are intoxicating
They promise it will be different
They promise it will get better

They promise you were overreacting

Of course they mean well, how could they not?

In their eyes you feel the clock begin to tick
Tick. They're waiting for you.
Tick. React or they'll forget about you.
Tick. It'll be too late for them to listen.
Tick. Their attention isn't forever.
Tick. They won't be able to see you much
longer.
Tick. Their attention is wavering.
Tick. They don't hear your screaming.
Tick. They don't understand your behavior.
Tick. They did nothing wrong.
Tick. It must be you.
Tick. Of course it's you.
Tick. It's always been you.
Tick.

Who else could it be?

Anti-Love

Getting up early
Forgetting the pizza
Writing me off
Staying ignorant
Placing bets
Gaslighting
Provocation
Ignoring
Disrespect
Laughing in my face
At my pain
At my passion
At my memories
At my rage
At my emotions
At my love
Turning a blind eye
Injustice
A coping mechanism
A scapegoat
An excuse
A place for poor behavior
A place for isolation
A place of non-acceptance
A place of not forgiving

A place of shame
A place of fear
An open mine field
A burning flame
A hidden dagger
A smoking gun
Held breath
Clenched knuckles
Bruised egos
Right and wrong
Suffering
Pain
Fear
Judgment

Love

A blanket wrapped around
Like a hug
Holding you in warmth
Peaceful energy
Spreading through you
Like the sun across the horizon
A calm ascension
Into a tepid demeanor
Housed in fragile glass
That heats from the inside out
Fortifying within
Until cannons couldn't breakthrough
Wars rage against walls
Made of steel
Echoes reverberate off the edges
The only enemy capable of winning
Is time moving against you
Even then
Ruins remain trapped in your heart
Waiting there until someone begins to excavate
As they search for space they might fit
They'll pick up some of the pieces
And place them in their own wall
As you build a place together
Working to stand the test of time

Anxiety

Anxiety builds from a deadly thought cycle
      Spiraling thoughts consume hope
Anxiety in my stomach feels like a black hole
      Waiting to tear me apart
Anxiety ignites my throat
      Leaving it scorching or gasping

The end of anxiety squelches thought
      Severing the connection between mind and body
The end of anxiety exhausts
      Extinguishing any breath of passion
The end of anxiety wrings the tension from my neck
      Leaving me broken and bruised

Doubt

Sometimes I let you win too easily
My emotions swirling
In your noxious tide pools
Thoughts festering in circles
Memories trudged up like the sand along the
bottom
Making everything murky

Inside that tidal pool of self-doubt
Everything seems so important
Whether the sentence I wrote above was great
Whether the moment I froze instead of speaking
my peace was bad
Whether I'll be able to show my face after a
little too much honesty and wine
Or even whether I should like myself or not
today

As the water stays isolated
It's harder to break the cycle
The little ecosystem you created
Fills in every crevice
Until it's like I'm not there at all

And it's frustrating

To feel like you're drowning in such shallow
waters
I know all I have to do is stand up
Or to wait for the tide to come back
Bringing a wash of crisp water

I don't stand up a lot
I believe you when you tell me I can't
I believe you when you tell me I shouldn't even
though I desperately wish to
I believe you when you tell me I'll fail
That I'll fall
That I'm stuck
That this is life
This is where I belong

Because I've made mistakes
I've said the wrong thing one too many times
I've spoken when I shouldn't have
I've hurt others
And I've been hurt
I've failed before
And I will fail again

So I know you're right
Of course you're right
Who was I to believe that I could stand
That I could face you
That I had anything that–

Ah, there's that wave
Your pool is diluted now
Your voice isn't as strong
You won't be able to hold me much longer
Because I have a secret
My greatest weapon against you

I know I can
And I know that I will

Frustration

Losing
Fainting
Pulsing

My mind scrambles
Inside a treasure trove of pressure
With each abrupt movement
I fear
Implosion

Frustration permeates
My thoughts
My energy
Until I become frustration
Over becoming myself

Imagine a world
With better balance
One I might visit
Staying isn't possible
My toxic cycle beckons me back
Like the family that led me there

How much easier it would be
To disappear

And escape this bleak
Winter
A cover up like the snow on rooftops

I used to think I was honest
Then I realized
I'm too afraid
Afraid to hurt people
That hurt me and others for sport

I've only just begun
To dodge the wrenches
They've bruised my insides
WIth the same force
My 7th grade gym teacher broke the glasses off
my face
Then laughed

I wish I could laugh as easily
That I might see the fun of the game
But I don't find pain to be very funny
Sorry AFV

Instead I have a resting bleak face
Made to show my disagreement
My discontent
The face becomes the ultimate target

Since my stance is already clear

Trying

You didn't know me before
But I wasn't always like this
I didn't always put this amount of effort
Into anything
My efforts stayed surface level
Minimum at best
Just enough to get by
And that had been enough

That's why this is different

I've been giving it my all
I've given it my all
I continue to give it my all
Yet the walls stay up
The gates stay locked

A dark cloud above barks down
"It won't be that easy this time"
So I tried even harder
"It will take more than that"
So I worked longer
"These doors aren't for everyone"
So I tried something new
"We need more"

So I did more
And more
And will continue to do more

You didn't know me before
But I never tried this hard

Condemnation

An entire town left me to die once
The isolation sliced through me
But instead of dying I wrote
In a way writing saved my life

Wish

I wish to weep with the sky
To wallow in the gray above
Melt into splashing puddles
Transform into the mist that just hits the rooftops
I wish to become a part of the cascading water

I wish to ascend with the evaporation
To join in the water cycle
Allow me to rinse and repeat
Transform me into the changing elements
I wish to become newly born and ever changing

I wish to be my own body of water
To splash when and where I see fit
Allow me to wash away the dirt on land
Transform me into the crystal clear mass
I wish to become one with the sea

Breathing

Sitting
Peacefully
Waiting
Watching
Breathing
Feeling

Serenity
In a moment

Calaminity
Mixed with
Calm

Circling
Swirling
Fusing
Together

Endless
Boundless
Approaching
Infinity
Staying finite

Exaggeration
Yet exact
Experience

Calm

The sea sits as vast and desolate as desert sand
Quiet and calm
Reflecting the state of mind
You feel with the lull of calm waves
Spurting along the side of the boat
Islands top the horizon
Like the oasis
Is it real or is it fake
The only proof
Hazy bumps breaking
The never ending sea

Storytelling

The portal to the otherworld
Gleams against the windowpane
Light beckons you forward
Convincing you of the promise
To leave this world and enter the next
The light tells you it's sweeter there
You'll be happier there
Entering the portal would strip
The dark cloud hanging over you

With each step forward
You believe the promise
Just a little bit more
At the threshold you almost smile
Yes you say
Strip me of this old life
So I might have a new one

The surface ripples beneath your light touch
Like a mold of jello
Your heart clamps up
Your hand pulls back
Your grandmother made jello that rippled
Will you remember her
Once you pass the threshold?

There's another light there inside of you
Buried beneath the darkness
It's battling for your attention
That small beacon of hope

Your smile dampens
Grandma died three years ago
How could you forget
You hadn't seen rippling jello since
Your father's attempts only slouched

The portal promises anew
No you will not forget
Child of this world
For we would grant you one memory
If you choose to cross this path
The portal's voice rippled across the jello
Making you giggle and step forward

And then pause
The pale blue in the jello'd portal
Is like the blue in your mother's eyes
Would you remember those eyes?

But how can I choose one memory
You ask the portal

The portal merely says

That is for you to decide

As you hold onto those wintry eyes
You remember your mother died
Five years before your grandmother
Darkness squeezes and suffocates
The little hope you had for this world

You must step through
It's the only way for life to get better

Once your foot disappears into the portal
You remember the bracers looped around your
brother's ankles
He needed them to walk
Your smile softens this time
He's still alive
He might need you
But then you remember you haven't spoken
For at least a year
If he needed you
Wouldn't he have called?

You sigh as you slip an arm through
Inside feels like the slime you played with as a
kid
Not like jello at all
Your father had hated that slime
Complained about how it left tracks

Like the trail a snail leaves as it slides across a
surface

You pause once more
You know he needs you
But since grandma
He hasn't been himself
He looks on you with distaste
As if he's ashamed you didn't make much of
yourself
As if that hadn't been so you could care for him

No you said
This world has done enough
I've done enough
You push through the membrane
And disappear from this world

2023

There's a moment of stillness
Between one year and the next
If you search for it
You won't find it
It will come to you though
In the brief quiet moment you allow yourself
For that moment
It's just you
And the air around you
The pause of chaos
Helps you breathe easier
Because you've done well
You'll continue doing well
So here's to a new year